PHILLIP RIXON

MONEY MASTER

The Ultimate Guide on How to Save and Make More Money, Learn Daily Tips on How to Motivate Yourself to Earn Money While Still Enjoying Life

Descrierea CIP a Bibliotecii Naţionale a României
PHILLIP RIXON
    MONEY MASTER. The Ultimate Guide on How to Save and Make More Money, Learn Daily Tips on How to Motivate Yourself to Earn Money While Still Enjoying Life / Phillip Rixon – Bucharest: Editura My Ebook, 2021
    ISBN

PHILLIP RIXON

MONEY MASTER

The Ultimate Guide on How to Save and Make More Money, Learn Daily Tips on How to Motivate Yourself to Earn Money While Still Enjoying Life

My Ebook Publishing House
Bucharest, 2021

TABLE OF CONTENTS

INTRODUCTION

When it comes to success in our professional and personal lives, few things aremore important than achieving a reasonable standard of living through wise personal finance decisions. Through our job choices, our saving, and our investing decisions, we determine what will be possible for us in the future, as well as when we can retire and how pleasant our retirement will be.

Indeed, this is all very important. However, without the right information available at our fingertips, we can often become paralyzed when it comes time to make those important decisions.

For instance, when it comes time to save, we might decide to put it off to anotherday. Or when it comes time to invest, we might jump the gun and it too early, even though we have outstanding debts that bear high interest rates.

In the rest of this audiobook, we will consider different tips that you can use to make these decisions the right way. Through this audiobook, I hope that you not only learn how to be frugal, how to save, and how to invest, but also how to steer your career (and exploit money making opportunities) in a way that will bring you closer to financial security and a broad sense of satisfaction with your life and your choices.

Tip #1: Buy products online.

One good way to limit impulse buying is to buy products online. It will allow you tomore easily comparison shop. And it will also prevent you from thinking that you have to buy, so that you don't have to drive somewhere else to make the purchase.

Tip #2: Comparison shop.

When making large purchases, you should always comparison-shop. By spending an extra 20-30 minutes to research your options, you could easily savehundreds or more.

Tip #3: Use coupons.

Whether you're grocery shopping or shopping for new electronics, using couponsis always a good way to go. So, from now on, stay in the habit of checking the newspaper and other local sources of coupons.

Tip #4: Use online coupon sites.

The Internet is now awash in online coupon sites. They collect and store couponsthat can be printed and used at various brick-and-mortar stores. Before you step out of your house, consider looking for coupons for your retail destination; and then putting them to use.

Tip #5: Enroll in rewards programs.

Grocery stores, clothing stores, and other retail stores now offer rewards programs. By signing up for a free membership, you can often gain access to a variety of coupons, discounts, and cash-back offers. Be sure to enroll in rewardsprograms that are offered at all of your favorite stores.

Tip #6: Create a shopping list in advance.

Eliminate junk food and foods that are inessential by creating a shopping list inadvance. At the end of the day, you'll walk away having spent less, and you'll also have all of the ingredients you'll need for weekly meals.

Tip #7: Wait for sales.

Some stores have regular sales. For instance, many stores hold sales after Christmas and other major holidays to sell off seasonal inventory. Take advantage of these predictable sales by delaying your purchases.

Tip #8: Limit entertainment spending.

Entertainment is important, but can often be obtained cheaply. From now on, limit your spending on entertainment until you have paid off your monthly bills and have saved a fixed portion of your income.

Tip #9: Learn how to do basic home repairs.

Learning how to do basic home repairs can save you a lot of money. Instead of calling a plumber or a carpenter, you can simply do the repairs yourself, saving you money and possibly also saving you the time it would take to negotiate the repairs.

Tip #10: Limit spending on expensive toys.

As a parent, it is your natural inclination to do what you believe is best for your child (and, sometimes, to simply spoil them). But when it comes to toys, more (and more expensive) is not always better. So, before you sink hundreds into the most fashionable toys, think twice about whether or not your kid might be better served by something less expensive.

Tip #11: Go to the movies less.

Instead of going to the movies all the time, stay home and rent a movie through your cable television service and procure your own snacks. Instead of spending $30-50, you'll spend a mere $10.

Tip #12: Substitute expensive food for cheaper foods.

Instead of dropping $200 per week on groceries, think hard about which items are luxuries and which items are actually important components of your weekly menu. Eliminate expensive items in favor of cheaper ones.

Tip #13: Buy store-brand products.

Store brand products are cheaper and frequently identical to name brand items. So, instead of immediately paying premium for the name brand product, consider at least trying the store brand once.

Tip #14: Use the slower shipping option.

When it comes to making online purchases, it is often tempting to opt for the fastest shipping. From now on, practice delayed gratification and opt for the slower, cheaper shipping option.

Tip #15: Buy gifts far in advance.

Many people wait until the last moment to buy gifts. As a result, they end up spending a lot of money the day or night before the event simply to get something nice. Instead of doing this, allow yourself weeks or months to pick up the product. Instead of rushing around the night before, you may stumble over it in a sale in the weeks leading up to the event.

Tip #16: Make your own gifts.

Candles, jewelry, and mix CDs can often make excellent, highly personalized gifts. Instead of purchasing a gift at the store, consider making one for your friend or family member.

Tip #17: Take public transportation.

Public transportation is often cheaper than owning, maintaining, and paying for gas for a car. Consider selling your car and making the switch.

Tip #18: Walk more.

Instead of driving your car small distances to the store and post office, consider walking to those places instead. Not only is it good for you, but it will save you money on gas and wear-and-tear.

Tip #19: Purchase a speed pass for tolls.

If the region you live in offers an automatic toll pass, purchase it. It may have a high upfront cost, but it will pay off in reduced tolls over time.

Tip #20: Purchase a pass for public transportation.

Purchase a pass to take the local train or subway system. In the long run, you'll save a lot of money by paying less each time you use public transportation.

Tip #21: Spend money on entertainment with high re-use value.

Instead of sinking money into video games and other forms of entertainment thatcannot be reused, instead focus on forms of entertainment that have a high re- usability factor. That is, try to get the most entertainment per dollar spent.

Tip #22: Make coffee or tea at home.

Buying coffee or tea at your favorite place can often be a nice experience. However, it is many times more expensive than making the same coffee or tea athome.

Tip #23: Stop smoking.

Smoking is both unhealthy and costly, so quit.

Tip #24: Reduce alcohol consumption.

Excessive drinking is both unhealthy and an unproductive activity. Cut thealcohol out of your budget and your life.

Tip #25: Replace incandescent light bulbs with compact fluorcscenls.

CFLs generate the light without the heat. For this reason, they use less energy.So make thc switch to CFLs.

Tip #26: Use the air conditioner and/or heater less frequently.

Air conditioners and heaters can use a great deal of electricity. So if you don'tneed to keep a room hot or cool, don't use them.

Tip #27: Hold a yard sale or setup a booth at a flea market.

Holding a yard sale or setting up a booth at a flea market will help you to a) get rid of the junk accumulating in your closets; and b) pick up some extra cash.

Tip #28: Base grocery shopping and meal plans around the availability ofcoupons.

Instead of using a fixed menu to buy groceries, create your menu to fit the availability of coupons for a particular week. This will ensure that you save asmuch as is possible each time you grocery shop.

Tip #29: Don't become addicted to spending.

Some of us gain pleasure simply by spending money. If you are one of those people, practice disciplining yourself by not blowing cash simply when you feeldepressed or down.

Tip #30: Meet with a financial planner.

A financial planner can help you to visualize your future; and how it will be shaped by savings decisions today. Do this as soon as possible, and get yourselfin a plan.

Tip #31: Shop for clothes at second hand stores.

Second hand stores often offer high-quality clothing for a mere fraction of the store price. Instead of spending all of your money on expensive brands at retail stores, consider getting the same items second hand.

Tip #32: Shop at bulk stores.

Bulk stores allow you to get massive amounts of products at a steep discount. If you want to save money in the long run, buying from these stores (and then storing the remaining quantities of the item) is the way to go.

Tip #33: Cook in bulk.

Cooking in bulk is another good way to save money and time. You can do this by producing a week's worth of food (or more) in a single session of cooking. You can then freeze the remaining food and re-heat it later in the week.

Tip #34: Limit spending on vacations.

When you do go on vacation, try to spend less. Instead of purchasing expensive hotel rooms, expensive dinners, and expensive drinks, try to reign things in and focus on being happy, rather than achieving happiness through luxury.

Tip #35: Go on cheaper vacations.

Go camping or take a "stay-cation." These can often be just as fun as a vacation to a far away place, but much cheaper.

Tip #36: Re-finance your house.

Since one of your largest monthly expenses is probably your mortgage, it is always a good idea to consider whether or not you could benefit from a re- finance. Do this periodically to make sure that you are getting the best rate.

Tip #37: Eat less meat.

Relative to the nutritional value it provides, meat is one of the more expensive components of your grocery spending. Consider cutting down on the amount youconsume.

Tip #38: Ask your credit card company to lower your interest rates.

Getting a lower interest rate on your credit card is often as simple as placing acall to the company. Get in the habit of doing this on a regular basis.

Tip #39: Pay off high interest rate debt.

Instead of paying down low-interest rate debt, pay down high-interest rate debt. This will reduce the overall amount you pay for debt servicing.

Tip #40: Ask to get fees waived.

Stores, credit card companies, and membership programs are often willing towaive fees if you claim that you will not use the service otherwise.

Tip #41: Move into a cheaper apartment or home.

If your rent or mortgage is unsustainably high, then move into a cheaperapartment or home.

Tip #42: Re-finance your car.

Consider re-financing your car. If your income has increased or your credit hasimproved, you might be able to get a lower rate.

Tip #43: Sell your car.

Cars are expensive. Consider selling yours and taking public transportationinstead.

Tip #44: Purchase a cheaper car.

Sell your car and buy a cheaper one - or perhaps one that gets better gasmileage.

Tip #45: Purchase additional razor blades, rather than entirely new razors.

Instead of buying a new razor, buy new blades, which are often now soldseparately.

Tip #46: Re-fill ink cartridges, rather than buying new ones.

Ink cartridges can now usually be re-filled using a toolkit and some toner. This is considerably less expensive than purchasing a new cartridge.

Tip #47: Re-finance your student loans.

If you are able to re-finance your student loans at a lower rate, do it.

Tip #48: Create a carpool for getting to work.

You need to get to work; and so do your co-workers. Create a carpool to save ongas and wear-and-tear.

Tip #49: Improve your gas mileage.

Use tricks to improve your gas mileage, such as using cruise control. A fewsimple tricks could save you $20 or more each week.

Tip #50: Add air to your car's tires.

Adding air to your car's tires (so that they are properly inflated) can improve yourgas mileage considerably.

Tip #51: Try to fix broken items, rather than buying new ones.

Fixing broken chairs, banisters, and other pieces of furniture or fixtures in your home is cheaper than buying new ones.

Tip #52: Take a bagged lunch to work.

If you're careful, you can take bagged lunches to work for a week for the sameprice you would spend in a single day if you were to go out to lunch.

Tip #53: Limit the frequency with which you dine out.

Dining out can be very expensive; and it is often easy to ignore exactly howexpensive it is. Try to do it less frequently.

Tip #54: Go to less expensive restaurants.

Not all restaurants are equally as pricey. Instead of blowing all of your cash on afancy night out, go to a cheaper one. It can easily be just as enjoyable.

Tip #55: Keep track of your debt.

Instead of paying attention to your minimum payments only, keep track of the total amount of debt you're holding, including student loans, credit card debts,and your mortgage.

Tip #56: Keep track of your savings and investments.

Many people make the mistake of ignoring their savings and investment. As a result, they reap small returns - if anything. They also face the risk of large losses during recessions and bubble bursts. Pay attention to where your moneyis invested and saved.

Tip #57: Get term, rather than permanent, life insurance.

Don't invest in life insurance. Instead, use it for its intended purpose: get terminsurance.

Tip #58: Use local exchange sites to find furniture.

Use local exchange sites to get furniture. In many cases, you will be able to findbed frames, couches, and shelves for free.

Tip #59: Don't store your credit card numbers online on sites.

Storing your credit card information on sites like Amazon makes it easy for you to buy things you don't need, so don't do it. Make it harder by not saving your information.

Tip #60: Do not spend up to your credit limit.

Spending up to your credit limit is rarely a good idea. Instead, try to stay as faraway from your limit as possible.

Tip #61: Avoid carrying a positive balance on any card that has a positiveinterest rate.

If a credit card bears a positive interest rate, you should pay it down immediately. Instead, transfer the balance to a card that temporarily has 0% APR or pay it off as soon as is possible.

Tip #62: Cut up your credit card.

While closing credit card accounts can often look like a negative on credit reports, no one will know if you cut up a card and threw it out. So cut up most ofyour credit cards and throw them out, but maintain your accounts.

Tip #63: Use a credit card for small purchases.

In order to improve your credit, use your card for small, daily purchases. Pay the balance off from these purchases each month.

Tip #64: Be mindful of teaser rates.

Most credit card companies will offer an initial teaser rate. Be mindful that this is not your permanent APR, but instead a temporary APR that is likely to change ina matter of months.

Tip #65: Never exceed your card's credit limit.

Exceeding your card's credit limit often comes with costly penalties. Avoid doingit.

Tip #66: Get a copy of your credit report.

At least twice a year, get a copy of your credit report to check for errors or forproblems you missed.

Tip #67: Ask your bank for better terms.

Call your bank and ask for better terms. This could help you to eliminate fees andget a higher interest rate.

Tip #68: Switch to a bank that has more ATMs in your area.

If you constantly find yourself paying fees to use other banks' ATMs, consider switching to a bank that offers more ATMs in your area.

Tip #69: Put a fixed fraction of your income into your savings.

Instead of thinking about how much to save each month, automatically put 10% of your income into savings each month. This is a good habit to develop earlier.

Tip #70: If you're planning to put money away for retirement, put it into amutual fund.

Put retirement savings into a mutual fund. Talk to your advisor to make sure themoney is invested well.

Tip #71: Invest your money in index funds.

Index funds are often cheapest to invest in and provide one of the best risk- adjusted returns. Consider putting retirement savings into index funds.

Tip #72: Cut down on extras on your cell phone plan.

Get rid of extras on your cell phone plan, including extended texting and dataplans.

Tip #73: Clean your car at home, rather than paying for it.

Instead of bringing your car to the car wash, grab a bucket of soapy water and abig sponge and get to work. You could save yourself a lot of money.

Tip #74: Get your tires rotated.

Rotating your tires can significantly improve your gas mileage and cut down on wear-and-tear. Make sure you do it regularly.

Tip #75: Start riding a bike.

Riding a bike is a good way to both get in shape and save money. Do it ratherthan driving your car everywhere.

Tip #76: Avoid clothes that require expensive upkeep, such as dry-cleaning.

Instead of opting for clothes that involve extensive dry cleaning, get clothes that do not require any special care. This will save you a considerable amount of money in upkeep.

Tip #77: Reduce your printing or print at the office.

Print less or print only when you can do it for free. This can easily save you $40 or more each month.

Tip #78: Sell your old clothes on eBay.

If you have extra clothing that no longer fits (or that you no longer like), sell it on eBay for some extra cash.

Tip #79: Use eBay to sell off old computers or computer parts.

If you have an old computer that you no longer use, sell it on eBay or at least take it apart and sell its parts, such as the professor, motherboard, and ram.

Tip #80: Use local exchanges to sell old furniture.

Sell your old furniture on local exchange sites. Even if you do not make a lot of money off of each piece, you can at least get someone to haul away your old furniture for free.

Tip #81: Bring someone who is good at bargaining next time you purchase a big-ticket item.

If you're planning to buy a big-ticket item, such as a house or a car or expensive jewelry, bring a good haggler with you. Make sure that this person does the talking and helps you to get a lower price.

Tip #82: Avoid purchasing store warranties.

Store warranties for electronics and other products are often rip-offs. Given the probability of replacement, the cost of the warranty is simply too high.

Tip #83: Use a clothesline, rather than your dryer.

It might seem embarrassing at first, but consider using a clothesline, rather than a dryer. You could save a great deal of electricity.

Tip #84: Clean off your refrigerator coils.

Cleaning off your refrigerator coils on a regular basis can significantly reduce the cost of refrigeration by improving its efficiency.

Tip #85: Use a bank that offers online banking services.

Being able to access your records online can make an important difference when it comes to saving and spending decisions, so use a bank that offers online records.

Tip #86: Pay your bills online.

Companies are often willing to reduce your bill if you pay online. Doing this for 3-5 companies can cut your bills back by $50 or more per month.

Tip #87: Enroll in automatic bill pay.

Similar to tip 111, companies also are often willing to pay more if you enroll inautomatic bill pay.

Tip #88: Purchase a coupon book for entertainment.

A coupon book is a book that contains hundreds of coupons for different products and events in your area. Consider paying the nominal fee of $10 or $20 to purchase one of these books.

30

Tip #89: Search out coupons for restaurants.

Many sites, including restaurant.com, offer large dining coupons. By joining andtaking advantage of these sites, you can eat for a fraction of the normal price.

That is for as little as $2, you can get a $20 meal.

Tip #90: Give up your gym membership and jog instead.

Instead of going to an expensive gym, give up your membership and get on aregular jogging routine.

Tip #91: Go to matinee showings of movies to save money.

Matinee showings of movies are frequently ½ to 2/3 the price of night showings.Consider switching your movie viewing times to save money.

Tip #92: Buy plane tickets far in advance.

In general, the further you purchase plane tickets in advance, the cheaper they will be. So don't wait until the last moment.

Tip #93: Don't accept quoted hotel prices. Instead, try to bargain.

Hotels are often willing to bargain if you're willing to ask. So don't stay silentunless you want to pay extra.

Tip #94: Bring snacks for flights.

Instead of paying $5, $10, $20, or more for snacks on flights, bring your ownsnacks and save some money.

Tip #95: When traveling, consider staying in a hostel.

Whenever you travel, consider staying in a hostel, rather than a hostel. You cansave as much as $80 per night if you're willing to stay in a communal room and share a bathroom.

Tip #96: Buy hygiene products in bulk online.

Buy hygiene products, such as toothpaste and mouthwash, online in bulk. Thiscan save you a lot of money in the long run.

Tip #97: Buy makeup online and in bulk.

Similar to tip 123, save money by purchasing your makeup online in bulk.

Tip #98: Avoid trends and fads.

Trends and fads in fashion and otherwise can be costly. Avoid them and insteadfocus on your long-term happiness.

Tip #99: Get dental work done by dental students.

Dental schools are often willing to perform dental work for cheap or at a discounted rate. Consider getting work done there, rather than at a dentist.

Tip #100: Get medical work done at a nearby university.

Getting medical work done at a university, rather than a doctor, is often a goodand low-cost alternative.

Tip #101: Housesit for extra cash.

One possible way to earn extra cash is to housesit. This simply entails finding someone who needs a house-sitter - and then to stay at their residence for a week or month while they are away on vacation.

Tip #102: Offer to babysit for neighbors and family members.

If you want to make money, one good way is to babysit for neighbors or for familymembers.

Tip #103: Cook more frequently.

Save money by staying in and cooking more frequently, rather than ordering foodor going to restaurants.

Tip #104: Use a high-yield savings account.

Instead of putting your money into a 0% return savings account, consider puttingyour money into a high-yield savings account.

Tip #105: Link your savings and checking account.

Linking your savings and checking accounts can help you to avoid overdraft fees.Check to see whether or not your bank offers this option.

Tip #106: Avoid enrolling in expensive banking account extras.

Instead of blindly accepting expensive extra that your bank offers, considerwhether or not you need each of them.

Tip #107: Pay your auto insurance in advance.

Consider paying your auto insurance in advance to avoid
the possibility of a lateor missed payment.

Tip #108: Make your car payments in advance.

Instead of making all of your car payments on time, make it
a goal to pay them inadvance - and to pay off your loan sooner
rather than later. If you have a flexibleloan, this will reduce the
amount of interest you pay in total.

Tip #109: Make an extra mortgage payment each year.

Paying your mortgage off sooner, rather than later, can
save you a considerableamount in interest payments.

Tip #110: Avoid credit cards with annual fees.

Don't get credit cards that have annual fees. Instead, look
only for cards that arefree to hold and use, as long as you pay off
your balance entirely.

Tip #111: Don't get rental car insurance.

Rental car insurance is often not worth it. Instead, simply
use your owninsurance.

Tip #112: Don't play poker or gamble.

Unless you have a lot of money to waste, opt not to participate in poker gamesunless the stakes are very low.

Tip #113: Try to find free or inexpensive parking, rather than settling for anexpensive garage.

If you're going somewhere, try to find free or inexpensive street parking, ratherthan opting for expensive garage parking.

Tip #114: Get routine maintenance done on your car.

You should always get routine maintenance done on your car, rather than waitingfor something to go wrong.

Tip #115: Always comparison shop for insurance.

Instead of taking the first quote that you get, comparison shop for auto insuranceand other types of insurance.

Tip #116: Install and use Skype.

For long distance phone calls, use Skype, rather than your phone. You could save hundreds of dollars if you make long distance calls frequently.

Tip #117: Weatherproof your home.

By weatherproofing your home, you can significantly decrease your heating andcooling costs in the long run.

Tip #118: Plant trees and bushes strategically to save on energy costs.

A few strategically placed trees and bushes can go a long way towards keepingyour house sheltered from wind and shaded from sunlight.

Tip #119: Purchase things used when possible.

Whenever possible, purchase used books, used clothes, and used furniture.You'll save a lot of money.

Tip #120: Make repairs to your car when feasible.

When it's feasible and safe, make minor repairs to your car yourself. For instance, if you have a scratch, go to the local car parts store and purchase the correct color spray paint to do the repair job yourself.

Tip #1: Purchase gifts after the holidays.

Instead of sending gifts on time, purchase them on sale after the holidayseason - and then send them out late.

Tip #158: Purchase textbooks used on half.com.

Use sites like half.com to purchase used textbooks at a sharp discount (if you area student).

Tip #160: Avoid paying for delivery. Instead, pick up the food.

Delivery is an expensive luxury. Unless you absolutely need it, pick up your foodinstead.

Tip #162: Purchase canned goods and other items that last longer.

Canned foods will significantly outlast their fresh food counterparts. Consider switching most items to canned food to ensure that food will last when you do not consume it immediately.

Tip #164: Don't take out the maximum in student loans.

Instead of taking out the maximum on student loans, take out no more than youneed.

Tip #165: Don't take out a loan simply because you qualify for it.

Just because you qualify for a loan does not mean that it is always a good idea totake it. Think carefully before you take one out.

38

Tip #167: Compare all loans you can get to the loans e-loan.com offers you.

When it comes to getting a loan, always compare what you're offered to what youcan get on e-loan.

Tip #168: Pay your bills on time to avoid late fees.

Don't ever miss a bill payment. One day might not seem like a big deal, but inreality, it can translate into tarnished credit and expensive fees.

Tip #169: Tutor students at the local high school to make money.

If you need to make money, consider working as a tutor for students at a schoolin your area. Focus on an area in which you have expertise.

Tip #170: Pick up a summer job, such as lifeguarding.

Pick up a summer job, such as working as a lifeguard. In addition to your normaljob, it will help you to make some extra cash.

Tip #171: Pick up a winter job, such as gift-wrapping.

Winter jobs and seasonal jobs can also make a nice addition to your normalemployment.

Tip #172: Add a part time job to your full time job.

If you are already working full time, consider picking up a part time job toaugment your income.

Tip #173: Meet with a career counselor.

Don't just think about the short term. Consider how you can improve your incomeprospects in the long run by talking to a career counselor and getting organized.

Tip #174: Go back to school to improve your career prospects.

Going back to school is one of the best ways to get ahead in life. If you're currently stuck in a dead-end job, consider going back to school for an MBA oranother practical degree.

Tip #175: Periodically apply to new jobs to see what types of offers you canget.

If you're wondering what type of salary the market might offer you, the best wayto find out is to submit applications. Do this on a regular basis to see whether ornot your prospects of moving up are good.

Tip #179: Start your own brick-and-mortar business.

Start your own brick-and-mortar business. Base it out of your house originally, but then move to a retail store once things get the chance to grow.

Tip #181: Reduce the costs that your current business incurs.

Another way to make more money is to cut costs at your existing business. Find ways to do things more efficiently and to reduce the costs of your inputs.

Tip #182: Get a roommate.

If you want to spend less on rent, get a roommate.

Tip #184: Go apartment hunting to find a better deal.

If your current apartment is too expensive, then spend more time searching for your next apartment, so that you can get a better price for the amenities you get.

Tip #185: Apply for insurance discounts, such as good student discounts.

Many insurance companies offer discounts for good students and for other reasons. When applicable, make sure you secure these discounts.

Tip #186: Move into a house with fewer (or no) unused rooms.

If you're living in a house with many extra rooms, consider moving to one that has fewer or no empty rooms to cut back on unnecessary mortgage and heatingcosts.

Tip #187: Get an energy audit.

An energy audit can help you to determine where you're wasting energy, so thatyou can adjust your behavior and save costs.

Tip #188: Try to minimize utility costs.

Wherever possible, cut down on utility costs by reducing energy and water use.

Tip #189: Take advantage of free financial counseling services.

Many non-profit organizations offer free financial counseling services. Takeadvantage of these if possible.

Tip #190: Go to the student aid office to get advice about your loans.

If you're a student, go to the financial aid office to get advice about your loans.Find out what types of loans are best for your particular situation.

Tip #191: Take advantage of local libraries.

Instead of buying books, videos, and CDs, borrow them from your local library.

Tip #192: Take advantage of parks.

Going to a park is a good alternative to more expensive forms of entertainment.

Tip #195: Use the same service for your Internet, cable TV, and phone.

Using the same service for your Internet, cable TV, and phone can save you a lotof money.

Tip #198: Get refurbished electronics, such as cell phones.

Instead of paying the full price for new electronics, purchase electronicsrefurbished to save money.

Tip #199: Use government-recommended energy-saving appliances.

When furnishing your kitchen and other rooms with appliances, consider purchasing only government-agency approved energy-efficient appliances to save on your utilities in the long run.

Tip #200: By generic OTC medications, rather than purchasing the brandname versions.

When purchasing over-the-counter medication, get generic versions, rather than name brands. They are chemically identical, but cheaper.

Tip #201: Take advance of employer pension and investment matchingprograms.

Many employers will match your 401(k) or other investment contributions. Take advantage of these programs by putting a larger portion of your income directly into your investment account.

Tip #203: Don't always submit insurance claims.

Before you submit an insurance claim, decide whether or not it is worth it. For instance, will the $500 you avoid paying out of pocket be less than the amount you will pay in higher premiums?

Tip #204: Apply for 0% interest credit cards.

Whenever possible, get a 0% APR credit card and transfer your high-interestcredit card debt to that card.

Tip #205: Eliminate expensive sources of debt.

Not all sources of debt are created equal. Eliminate the ones that incur massive financing charges by paying them off first or by taking out a consolidation loan toeliminate them.

Tip #206: Go to a health fair to get reduced-cost services.

Health fairs often offer steeply discounted rates on physical check-ups, blood- pressure checks, and other routine medical procedures. Take advantage of theseto save some money.

Tip #207: Don't go to the ER or use other high-cost medical services.

Instead of going to the Emergency Room, schedule an appointment with a doctor. This could save you hundreds of dollars.

Tip #209: Look for free healthcare services.

Next time you see a free health clinic or some other free health care service, takeadvantage of it.

Tip #210: Argue insurance claims against you.

Next time you are involved in a car accident, work hard to state your case. Do notsimply allow the insurance companies to hear the other person's version of the story.

Tip #212: Purchase new eye glasses whenever deals become available.

From time to time, companies will offer steep discounts on eye-glasses. Whenever these become available, take advantage of them to secure a new pairof glasses.

Tip #213: Do teeth-whitening at home with store-bought products, rather than paying for professional services.

Rather than paying for professional teeth-whitening services, purchase a store at a convenience store and use it at home. This can save you hundreds of dollars and produce comparable results.

Tip #214: Make use of dollar stores.

While much of the inventories of dollar stores are frivolous items, some things are truly useful. Look for these items and save.

Tip #215: For home-cooked meals, avoid pre-cut foods and chop the foodsat home instead.

Purchasing foods before they are cut will save you a large chunk of money. Getin the habit of doing this.

Tip #216: Pay attention to receipts.

When you're at the register, pay attention to each item's price as it is rung in.Also, check the receipt after you're finished to make sure you were charged correctly for each item.

Tip #219: Setup an eBay store.

One way to gain a reputation on eBay and to speed along your sales is to create a store. Do this to sell your bargain bin merchandise.

Tip #220: Buy products at government auctions and resell them on eBay.

If you want to make money without putting down a large investment, consider buying products at a steep discount at government auctions; and then resellingthem on eBay.

Tip #221: Use inexpensive methods to promote your business, such asonline advertising.

Instead of using expensive promotional methods, try to use targeted advertising for your brick-and-mortar business, such as online, contextual ads.

Tip #222: Advertise your business or services through flyers with rip-offnumbers.

Advertise your brick-and-mortar business or your services through flyers with rip-off numbers.

Tip #223: Locate scrap metal and sell it at a scrap yard.

Scrap yards are often willing to pay hundreds of dollars for large pieces of aluminum or other metals. Consider using sites like Craigslist to locate pieces of scrap metal, so that you can pick them up and resell them.

Tip #224: Offer to drive co-workers and friends to mutual locations if theyare willing to cover part of the gas.

Whenever possible, try to setup a carpool with your friends and co-workers. Thiswill allow you all to share the cost of gas and of wear-and-tear on the car.

Tip #225: Create and sell content online.

If you're good at writing, consider writing articles, ebooks, or reports - and thenselling them online.

Tip #226: Work through Elance.com as a consultant.

If you want to make money online, consider working as a consultant in your areaof expertise on Elance.com.

Tip #227: Find freelance writing projects online.

Find freelance projects on Elance.com and other sites to make money in yourspare time.

Tip #229: Offer to sell your friends' and neighbors' stuff on eBay for a smallcommission.

Know someone who has some extra junk lying around in her home? Offer to sellit online on eBay for a small commission.

Tip #233: Sell individual stock photos.

Take photographs of everyday things, such as sunsets, sunrises, buildings, animals, and nature scenes. Sell these individual photos on a stock photo site.

Tip #234: Sell stock photo lightboxes.

If you're a good photographer, create a lighbox of photos for a particular themeand then sell it on a stock photo site.

Tip #235: Work as a blogger for pay.

Using Elance.com or another site, find a site administrator who needs a full timeblogger. If you're a good writer who can come up with clever blog entries, this is a good way to make money.

Tip #240: Invest in "virtual real estate."

Instead of investing all of your savings in stocks and bonds, put some of it intodomains, fully developed sites, or other forms of virtual real estate.

Tip #251: Create an ebook and sell it.

If you're an expert on a topic and a good writer, create an ebook and sell it onlinefor a relatively cheap price.

Tip #253: Sell a hardcover book.

If you already have a ebook that is selling well, consider converting it into ahardcover book via a self-publishing site; and then resell it.

Tip #256: Create an email list.

Whether or not you own a website, consider creating an email list; and thenmarketing products and services to that list.

Tip #257: Pitch to your email list.

If you have an email list, sell affiliate products to your list for a commission orcreate new products to sell to it.

Tip #258: Sell ads on your email list.

In addition to pitching affiliate products and your own products to email lists, consider allowing other business owners to pay to advertise on your email list. Ifyou have a large list, this can be quite profitable.

Tip #260: Work as a copywriter for an Internet marketer.

Find an Internet marketer in need of a copywriter either on warriorforum.com. Offer to do the copywriting work at a steep discount.

Tip #262: Work as a freelance pet-sitter for families in your area.

Find families in your area who need a pet-sitter. Offer to take the job.

Tip #263: Sell professional dog-walking services.

Consider selling dog-walking services to families in your area. This can be very profitable - especially if you are able to walk several dogs at the same time.

Tip #264: Do freelance landscaping work, such as lawn mowing.

Pick up odd jobs as a landscaper. Offer to mow lawns, trim the grass, and killweeds.

Tip #265: Shovel or plow driveways.

In the winter, offer to shovel or plow driveways. This will work especially well if you have a plow and a truck, as you can pick up an easy $20 by plowing a shortdriveway.

Tip #266: Get a part time job at a department store and take advantage ofthe discount.

Department stores often offer large discounts to employees. Get a job at one ofthem and take advantage of the discount to purchase everything cheaper.

Tip #267: Work as a caddy at a golf course.

While working as a caddy may seems like a menial job, it can often generate good connections in the process. Consider doing it at your local golf course.

Tip #268: Seek out joint venture partners.

If you have a business or a product, seek out joint venture partners to promoteyour business, to franchise it, or to expand it along some profitable dimension.

Tip #269: Save 10% of your income.

If you want to save money, commit to putting at least 10% of your income away initially. Over time, consider increasing this amount.

Tip #270: Put your saved money into long-term investments, so that youcan't withdraw it.

If you have a hard time preventing yourself from spending money, use investment accounts that incur fee if you withdraw money early. This will give youan incentive not to cheat.

Tip #271: Setup money to be automatically withdrawn from your bank account and placed in a mutual fund or investment account.

In order to facilitate saving, setup your bank account so that money is automatically sent to an investment account after your paycheck is deposited.

Tip #272: Don't carry cash.

Having cash available will make you more likely to spend it. Instead, try to carryvery little cash.

Tip #273: Set goals and follow through.

When it comes to saving, setting goals is vital. Decide where you want to go,commit to it, and then follow through.

Tip #274: Buy books and clothes from thrift stores and resell them online.

Go to thrift stores where second hand furniture and articles of clothing are sold.Buy them at a steep discount and then resell them on sites like eBay and Amazon.

Tip #275: Provide proofreading services for students.

If you're a good writer, consider offering proofreading services for college students for a nominal fee. You can do this at a local university or by seeking out students on sites like Elance.com.

Tip #276: Work as a paid forum poster.

If you already like posting on forums, consider taking a job as a forum poster. Usually, you will be assigned to a niche and to a set of forums; and you will thenneed to meet a certain quota for forum posts each day.

Tip #277: Become a paid site administrator.

If you have good programming and site management skills, consider becoming asite administrator for a number of different small Internet-based companies. You can find these jobs through freelance sites and on forums.

Tip #284: Work in freelance data entry.

Data entry is a simple job that usually does not require any high-level skills. Consider picking up data entry jobs on Elance.com to do when you have sparetime.

Tip #288: Design and sell site logos.

If you have knack for website design, consider designing and selling logos forwebmasters on sites like sitepoint.com.

Tip #289: Sell clip art.

Similar to tip 288, but with clip art.

Tip #290: Sell customized avatars for forums.

Similar to tip 288, but with forum avatars.

Tip #292: Eliminate credit card debt before investing.

When it comes to investing, try to eliminate all of your credit card debt beforeputting money into investment. Since the interest rate on your credit cards is higher than your return, the best investment you can make is to eliminate it.

Tip #293: Eliminate debt in order of the size of the interest rate.

When you eliminate credit card debt, do it in order of the size of the interest rate.Highest interest rates should go first.

Tip #296: Stop scaling your consumption up when your income rises.

When your income rises, add more to your income, rather than to yourconsumption.

Tip #297: Practice frugality in all your choices.

In all choices in your life, practice frugality. Try to look for a cheap, but good-enough option, rather than the most expensive option.

Tip #298: Don't try to "keep up" with your friends.

Stop trying to "keep up" with your friends by spending more. Instead, accept that the newest, largest TV and a new car simply may be out of your financial reach.

Tip #299: Live simply.

Practice living simply and finding enjoyment in simple, inexpensive activities. Donot rely on money to bring happiness.

Tip #300: Create a budget and follow it carefully.

Instead of allowing ad-hoc spending to rule your life, create a monthly budgetand follow it carefully. Unless you have a very good reason, do not deviate.

Tip #301: Budget with your spouse.

If you're married, budget jointly with your spouse. Instead of shifting money between you, figure out how much you have together and determine your financial decisions jointly.

Tip #302: Update your budget at least once monthly.

At least once a month, re-consider the budget you have created and decide whether you have allocated the right amounts to the right categories. If it is unrealistic or puts too much into a particular category, re-adjust your budget.

Tip #303: Use the lowest octane fuel permitted for your car by your owner'smanual.

If your car does not require high-octane fuel, then don't use it. It does nothing tohelp your car and is more expensive.

Tip #304: Shop around for cheaper homeowner's or renter's insurance.

Don't simply take the first option you get for renter's or homeowner's insurance. Instead, try to find a company that offers the right type of coverage and at a priceyou can afford.

Tip #305: Avoid taking out home equity loans.

Home equity loans are a good way to ensure that you never pay off your mortgage and never own your home. Unless you need to take one out to covermedical bills or something similarly important, do not get one.

Tip #306: Periodically shop around for a re-finance.

From time-to-time, look around to re-finance your mortgage. You could save a tremendous amount in monthly payments through a tiny interest rate reduction.

Tip #307: Adjust your tax withholding to give yourself a raise.

In many cases, your tax withholding will be too high. Take the time to adjust it, sothat you can have the money now - rather than when you pay taxes.

Tip #308: Switch to paperless notifications for your bills.

Many companies will take $5-10 off of your bill when you use paperlessnotifications exclusively. Do this with all of your bills.

Tip #309: Use the library, rather than purchasing new books.

Instead of buying new books, use the local library or the university library tocheck out the book.

Tip #310: Look for DVDs at the library, rather than renting them.

Use the local library to borrow DVDs, rather than paying $5-10 to rent them for afew days.

Tip #311: Sell your car and use an e-carpooling connection service to get towork.

Use an e-carpooling service to find rides to work. Usually, you can do this withouthaving a car, as long as you are willing to pay for gas.

Tip #312: Check to see whether or not your checking account is insured bythe Federal government.

If the Federal government insures your account, then you will not be at risk oflosing money if anything happens to the bank, which you are using to save.

Tip #313: Shop around for the savings account that offers the highest yieldat little to no risk.

Most savings accounts bear little to no risk. Take advantage of this by finding the savings account that offers the highest return.

Tip #314: As you get older, shift more of your money from stocks to bonds.

As you get closer to retirement, move your money away from risky equities and into government and AAA-rated bonds. Your average return will be smaller, but you will hedge against losing a large portion of your net worth with few working years left to recover it.

Tip #315: Set aside money for savings before you allocate money to anyother budget category.

Consider saving first and spending later. Intuitively, this might seem backwards, but in reality, it is an excellent habit to develop.

Tip #316: Develop good saving habits.

Get in the habit of putting extra money into your savings whenever you have it, rather than finding ways to blow it.

Tip #317: Start saving early.

Instead of waiting until you are in your 30s or 40s to start saving for retirement, start doing it while you're young. Compound interest will make this investment deciding pay off.

Tip #318: Get a free savings account.

Instead of getting a savings account that requires various fees and payments, look for a free account. In most situations, if you are keeping at least $100 in the account, you can do it for free.

Tip #319: Try to negotiate a lower rate in exchange for using direct deposit.

Some banks will give you incentives to use direct deposit and electronic transfers, rather than check-cashing. See if you can use this as a bargaining chipto negotiate lower fees.

Tip #320: Credit cards that offer rebates or rewards might not always be thebest option.

Even if a card offers 3% cash back, it might not be the best card for you. Consider other dimensions of the card, such as its APR and its annual fee.

Tip #321: Set saving goals.

Decide how much you want to save before you hit 30, 40, and 50. Make specificgoals and try to keep them.

Tip #322: Execute your saving goals.

When it comes to your saving plan, execution is key. It is one thing to say "I wantto have at least $60,000/yr to live off of after I retire" and it is another thing to make it happen. Don't let yourself drift too far when trying to execute your savings plan.

Tip #323: Set goals for your business.

If you own a business, set goals for its growth and development. Instead of letting things drift, force them to move in a favorable direction.

Tip #324: Set personal finance goals.

When it comes to personal finance, keep yourself on track by creating goals. Forinstance, set a goal to create and stick to a monthly budget. Or set a goal to not miss a single bill (or pay late) for an entire year.

Tip #325: Periodically assess how well you have kept your goals.

On a regular basis, decide whether you have lived up to your business and financial goals. If you're doing poorly, ask why. And also think about how you canimprove.

Tip #326: Stay consistent with your saving habits.

From time to time, we convince ourselves that we don't need to save when our lives become financially difficult. However, in reality, we are setting ourselves upto cycle between good and bad saving behavior.

Tip #327: Find a better job.

One important way to increase your income is simply to find a better job. If you'vebeen working at the same place for 10 years and have received few raises, consider leveraging your experience and switching to a job that is willing to pay you more.

Tip #328: Don't buy things you cannot afford.

In general, a good way to save money is to avoid buying things you cannot afford. If you can't afford a big screen TV without paying for it with credit, thendon't buy it.

Tip #329: If you're a student, buy paperback versions of textbooks.

As a student, textbooks can be incredibly expensive. For this reason, you should try to hunt down paperback and pre-owned versions on half.com, Amazon.com, and other book resellers.

Tip #330: Buy electronic versions of tangible products.

If a product comes in both a tangible and electronic form, opt for the electronicform. It will often be considerably cheaper.

Tip #332: Recycle your old clothing into things you need.

If you have old clothing that you do not wear, consider recycling it into somethingyou need, such as a wall decoration, a wallet, or a bracelet.

Tip #333: Use old decorations in new ways.

A vase that holds flowers can become a vase that holds decorative sand orbeads. Be creative in using old decorations to make new ones.

Tip #334: Use book trade-in websites to get new books.

Use a book trade-in site to exchange your old books that you've already read fornew ones. This is an excellent alternative to constantly purchasing new books.

Tip #338: Use a powerstrip with your electronics in your entertainmentcenter.

Use a powerstrip with all of the electronic devices in your entertainment center.When not in use, click off the power strip.

Tip #339: Shut the water off while you brush your teeth.

Saving water can reduce your utilities bills. So next time you brush your teeth,remember to shut off the water, rather than letting it run.

Tip #340: Spend less time in the shower.

As with tip 339, try to conserve water by spending less time in the shower.

Tip #341: Bottle your own water.

Instead of purchasing expensive bottled water, fill a water bottle up using the tapin your house.

Tip #342: Use rechargeable batteries.

Instead of constantly buying new batteries, purchase rechargeable batteries,which will last for many cycles.

Tip #343: If you have a young child, use cloth diapers.

If you have a young child, consider using cloth diapers, rather than plasticdiapers to save on costs.

Tip #346: Take advantage of free promotional offers from local businesses.

When businesses offer free food and drinks or free promotional productions, takeadvantage of these offers.

Tip #347: Water your lawn less frequently.

To save on your utilities bills, try to water your lawn less frequently.

Tip #348: Use powdered juice mixes, rather than soda.

Instead of purchasing bottles of soda, drink tap water mixed with powdered juice. This will be considerably less expensive.

Tip #349: When traveling, stay at a friend's house, rather than a hotel.

If you're planning to go on vacation or to visit friends or family, plan to stay at someone's house, rather than in a hotel. You could save hundreds on a week-long trip.

Tip #350: Use couchsurfing.com to find places to stay while traveling.

If you don't have anyone to stay with on your next trip, use couchsurfing.com to locate people who are willing to host visitors in their homes.

Tip #351: Keep an eye on social media sites, such as Twitter, for limitedtime offers.

Many businesses, including retail stores, airlines, and others, offer limited timeoffers on Twitter. By taking advantage of these brief offers, you can save hundreds of dollars.

Tip #352: Fill surveys to get free stuff.

Today, many companies offer free products and cash in exchange for filling outsurveys. Do this wherever possible.

Tip #353: If dissatisfied with a product or service, contact the company.

If you are unhappy with a product or service, you could consider contacting the company who produced it. In many cases, they will be willing to offer a refund orfree products.

Tip #354: Try samples of new products before purchasing.

Before you make a large purchase, try out a free sample. For instance, drive a car before you buy it. Or taste-test an expensive wine or food before you purchase large quantities of it.

Tip #355: Print photos at a local store, rather than using an expensivephoto printer.

Instead of purchasing an expensive photo printer, print your photos at a localprint shop. Typically, this is cheaper than paying for photo printer ink.

Tip #357: Contact your TV and Internet provider for the most recentbundles and deals.

If you feel like you might be paying too much for your TV and Internet, contactyour cable company to find out about the most recent deals. You may find thatsimilar packages are now available at a much lower price.

Tip #358: Don't let your batteries for electronic products drain down to 0%.

Do not allow batteries for your electronics to drain down completely on a regularbasis. This will decrease the long term total life of the battery.

Tip #360: When grocery shopping, look for "day old" food that is now onsale.

Day old food, such as bread, is often sold at a sharp discount in the grocery store. Look for this section to get big discounts.

Tip #361: Take your pets to a non-profit vet.

Non-profit vets often offer considerably lower rates. Seek one out before you goto for-profit vets.

Tip #363: In the winter, seal windows with plastic wrap to save money onheating.

Insulating your home better can drastically reduce your energy costs. One way you can do this is by covering windows with plastic.

Tip #364: Only heat or air-condition the part of the house you are using.

If you're not using a room, then don't pay to heat or air-condition it. Instead, shutoff the heater or air conditioner.

CONCLUSION

You've now read tips for living frugally, saving your money, making more money, and investing your money wisely. Only you know which of these tips can transform your life, and which are best ignored.

So keep this document close, choose your tips selectively and wisely; and then actually stick to advice in the tip once you have decided to follow it.

When it comes to making good personal finance decisions, a plan is important. But the plan alone will not get you to your destination without clean execution, hard work, and tough decisions.

And with that, I leave you to grow your wealth, to achieve financial security, and to become happy with your life and your decisions.

Printed by Libri Plureos GmbH in Hamburg, Germany